NATURAL WONDER

Victor Klimoski

Prior Avenue Publication □ 2019

Cover Consultant: D.J. Vail
Cover Photo: Sossusveli, Nambia by John Gorton

ISBN: 9781093635416
Imprint: Independently published by KDP

Acknowledgements

While no one can write for you, we seldom end up writing in isolation. The responses of people to individual poems, the comments of a writing group (if you are fortunate to have one), and the feedback from brave souls who agree to do a critical review of a completed manuscript all provide ways of seeing your words from a more objective point of view. Ann Glumac and Sam Rahberg, both accomplished writers in their own right, performed a noble service by reading these poems carefully and telling me the truth. Their comments strengthened poems that were wavering. They helped me find my way to better words, better lines, and, in some instances, the difficult decision to remove poems I proposed to include. And my friend and colleague, Cathy Slight, who agreed to do a final proofreading of the manuscript, also asked questions about some of the poems that in fact led to yet more fruitful revision. I am grateful for the generosity of these three in particular for sharing their talent in bringing Natural Wonder *to completion.*

The Pennsylvania Poetry Society awarded "Natural Wonders" a first place in its 2019 competition. The Missouri State Poetry Society awarded third place to "Mistaken Identity" in its 2019 winter contest.

*

Nature is ever at work building and pulling down, creating and destroying, keeping everything whirling and flowing, allowing no rest but in rhythmical motion, chasing everything in endless song out of one beautiful form into another.

John Muir (1838-1913)

*

Natural Wonders

The Earth is an endless tale
told anew day after day
with wonders so grand
they can leave us speechless -
the faithfulness of sunrise,
the steadfastness of the wind,
the deliberation of crows
       at first light,
a cantata of bees at work
in fields of crimson clover,
the castanet dance of crickets
across furrowed rows of hay.

We take for granted the oratory
that booms from a summer storm
as lightning scrawls its name
across a blackened sky.
Weary when dusk comes,
we fall into the arms
of the purpling silence
as day seeps away,
leaving the land hushed
under the soft narration
       of a starlit night.

Brilliant Morning

This brilliant morning,
is a new text.
What was written in dust
has been washed away.
Each leaf, each blade of grass,
shimmers a fresh message.
Even the brooding pond
now shines bright and clear,
in quiet proclamation.

This brilliant morning
longs for a song, a canticle
whose gentle cadence
slides across the slick blue lake
and slips into the forest.
There every tree joins the chorus,
passes the song branch to branch.
Deer, hearing it, pause,
count the beat and then leap,
twigs snapping to the rhythm.

This brilliant morning
makes us stop midsentence,
forget last night's argument,
and turn, hearts racing,
toward the source of light.

Surprise

We need moments when we taste
the surge of sweet surprise
as a grayed world splits open,
and rays of light,
like a crystal held to a flame,
spill across a darkened sky.
Or we might see a red bird,
its feathers fringed with fire,
and stop,
lost for words.

The Cycle of Time

June's extravagant light
steadily declines,
taking with it the memory
          of summer's first promise.
We grow accustom to the change,
know this cycling of seasons
is the way we track time,
its bold line threading together
days and months that pass
in the blink of an eye.

The thinning of light,
the thickening of dark,
shift our moods,
as what we know passes
and what is to come
lies veiled in a mystery
we feel in our bones.

Still Life

Ardara, County Donegal

The buttery light of dawn

drifts slowly across the bedroom floor,

signaling the night ghosts

to take their leave.

Soon the very walls glow,

bands of golden sunbeams

smoothing chipped paint

and ragged strips of wallpaper.

One beam catches on a framed image

of a white, thatched-roof cottage

nestled on a steep green hill.

And memory climbs that hill

on a perfect day in June,

past rough stone walls

and through patches of bog grass,

their feathery heads bobbing gaily.

Far below, a small stream

winds down from Glengesh Pass,

its banks lined with broom and gorse,

turlough, goat's beard, and ragwort.

As the sun turns westward,

the amber light of afternoon

casts creamy shadows down the hill,

the thatch on Rose Cottage

suddenly saffron and claimed forever.

This Day Before Us

On any one day,
on a day like this
when the sun sweeps back
the last traces of night,
the heavy dew of August
ripples across trimmed lawns.
On a day like this,
it is time to begin again.
We have lingered too long
under the traces of regret,
plowing furrows too shallow
for the harvest we imagined.

Today, we will look up,
breathe in the morning air
and open our hearts
to what lies just beyond
the fading sea of dew.

Signs and Wonders

If it is true about birds,
that their frenzy at dawn
is their praise for creation,
we humans must be chastened
at our own tied tongues.

We may notice trees
in their fall promenade
too flashy to ignore,
or pause over a rosebush
imperial in morning's light.

Too often, we simply pass by,
duty blinkering our eyes,
our minds replaying an argument
from yesterday or last year
that always ends the same.

If we can re-teach our hearts
to leap as sunrise sets ablaze
a hillside of windrowed hay,
we might speak in tongues
a prophecy for Beauty.

Fog

Fog softens the world,

feathers its sharp edges

and smooths blemishes

so stark in daylight.

Fog casts a mysterious veil,

leaving everything porous,

ghostly and evanescent.

What we see is obscured –

a shadow, an outline,

a thing we almost recognize

      but faintly.

Fog teaches humility,

tempers quick judgments.

It forces us to slow down,

look twice, more intently.

The landscape once familiar

is suddenly new terrain,

and we, becoming attentive,

find ourselves explorers.

Seeing Beyond

Walking along a stony beach,
your eye might gaze
across the plain of water,
its secrets cupped
in the tips of white waves.
Or your ear might attune
to gusts of wind, rushing
from boughs of white pine
to stir gulls from their sleep.
Or you might feel drawn
to one particular stone
in this congregation of stones.
You read its markings
as a hieroglyph of Creation,
a story of beauty as sharply etched
as the thin black line separating
     sky from water,
the stone as mysterious
as the arc of time
         across space.

The River: A Teaching

Some study the river closely.
They can name its origins,
its length, the route it travels.
They recite its tributaries,
its lineage, the towns
it created and the tribes
who used its sacred name.
They know everything
there is to know about the river,
but they have never gotten wet,
never let the water wash over them
or feel the way it changes moods,
captures the sky, or sighs.
The river remains a curiosity,
a geological puzzle.
But they don't revere the river,
come to it for instruction,
hear its lessons, let it yoke
mind and body together
in deep assurance that all
is beginning,
            all is moving,
        forward.

Determining Authority

We are so sure
we are the ones
who shape a day.
Yet the Sun rises
of its own accord,
and winds move
in currents known
to them alone.
Earth turns silently,
pursuing its orbit
without map or compass.

Yet, in the blue spruce
just outside my window,
a cardinal sings a psalm
it composed long ago,
long before I was born
to fret and wonder
how I might make
the Sun rise, the Earth spin,
a bird sing on cue.

Tanka For An Early Spring

A small red-beaked bird
huddles in lush evergreen boughs,
braced against the wind,
its head tucked under its wing,
its beak a flame of hope.

Yellow Pear

A perfect yellow pear,
one crisp green leaf on its stem,
sits in a white porcelain bowl
on the kitchen window ledge.

The sun is setting and its light,
filtered through a skein of branches,
animates the pear, its leafy cap,
even the simple white bowl.

The pear begins to glow,
the bowl becomes translucent,
and somewhere in the house
waltz music fills the air.

Reverie

The stubbled cheek of a cornfield

spreads across the countryside,

ending at a stand of oaks,

a matronly party of *grande dames,*

their dresses of royal red and purple

rustling like fine, old silk.

Even under leaden skies,

such beauty draws a gasp

and a deep desire to keep

this portrait unchanged

     when snow comes,

     as memory dims.

End of Summer

Each leaf swirls downward
as trees open long elegant limbs
to receive the wind's silky touch
winding through their branches,
a caress the trees nearly forgot
but recall in an instant,
like a first kiss lingering
on lips still pursed.

And Still Tomorrow

The sumac are grieving,
their once brilliant fronds
drooping sadly to the ground.
A day ago they caught sunbeams
in their tiny red fingers
that, now mottled,
fall one by one by one.

This signal of change,
catches me off guard,
as though my bones
did not bear its knowledge.
For the turning of a season
now accents the pace of change,
its leaving behind what's undone.

Soon the sumac will be naked,
their gray bones clicking in the breeze.
But deep in their roots,
in their dark solitude,
they know they will rise again,
lush and green and filled
                    with sunlight.

Winter Solstice

Earth grows gaunt and gray,
as it fasts from light,
and the way forward darkens
from losing track of time.
I hurry through gathering shadows,
my heart quickening with my pace.
When I see the light in the window,
I pause, fearing the hour too late,
the host annoyed by my delay.
I move forward slowly,

     hesitate at the door,

    turn to go, then turn back,

my fears outdone by a long journey
and its kindled need
for the fire of companionship,
and conversation,

     soft and familiar.

…the world offers itself to your imagination,

calls to you like the wild geese, harsh and exciting --

over and over announcing your place

in the family of things.

Mary Oliver (1935-2019), "Wild Geese"

Serenity: A Recipe

Do nothing.
Sit in one place.
Quiet your mind,
sending anxiety
    out for fresh air.
In this calmed space,
watch a beam of light -
    thin, fragile, yet charged
    with the Sun's power -
as it dances across the floor
    changing everything,
    changing you.

To See As A Child

To see as a child sees,
to see the world as it is,
as it presents itself
in its native garb,
we must quiet our minds,
and our disappointment
over perfection's failed arrival.
       Instead, let imaginations
wander into the fields of beauty
so as each day begins,
       before duty beckons,
we might kneel in the grass,
bend down to the Earth
kissing it gently, feeling
its love enter our mouths,
       our eyes,
          our waiting hearts.

Ready, Set, Change

We are ready to set out
when the way seems straight,
when the plan is clear,
when we're always in shade,
when rest is well-paced,
when the weather is mild,
when companions are cheerful,
when our shoes do not pinch,
when thirst and hunger vanish,
when there's beauty all around,
when there are few surprises.

But what we often find
is clumsy back-tracking,
running out of supplies,
the fear of being lost
with no sure route home.
This is our journey,
the one that finds us.
So tighten your laces,
grab a sturdy stick,
and keep a song handy -
as well as knowledge
of which berries
are safe to eat.

Calamity

In the calamity of daily life
and the chaos it evokes,
we too easily forget
how wide the universe,
how narrow our vision.

A helpful practice each day
is to take the world's pulse,
feel its heartbeat
as it pumps fire
into the veins of matter,
microscopic and galactic.

Anxiety may not disappear,
fear may still whisper,
but we may come to learn
how fate rests not
in singular endurance
but in symbiotic flow.

Perspective

Six people
on six chairs
look upon
the same painting.
Each describes
what they see –
six images,
each one right,
each incomplete,
but together
opening hearts
so each can see truly
what only can be seen
with good companions.

Shadow

Can you lose your shadow,
outrun it as you round
the corner of the house?
Is it attached to your heels,
or stitched to your soul
even in dark of night?
What does your shadow know,
this dutiful, faceless ghost?
Does it carry your secrets
deep in its pockets lest light
reveal your scrapes and scars?
Is it a faithful companion,
the one who, knowing you best,
stays close no matter what,
and is ready to take the lead
when you've lost zeal to go on?

Embracing Stillness

Stillness requires silence
and, by an act of will,
finding a center point,
as you do the horizon
when crossing an angry sea.

When you gain your bearing,
calm the turmoil of thoughts,
you are ready to hear
what you too soon miss
in the squall of daily life.

Passage of Time

The fresh face of the New Year
is suddenly the bent back of Autumn.
The child in the crook of my arm
is now holding her own child
who, as I turn, leaves for college.
The face in the mirror is a map
laid out in spots and lines,
and my mother's hands now dangle
at the end of my wrists,
their skin thin and crêpey.
Joints ache, energy wanes,
and I think more often of death.
Time is as unstoppable
        as it is indifferent.

Passage of time alone
is just one version of a life,
for anyone's story comes
in different versions, each
helping to find a place
for what's been gained,
        left undone,
        or ended in defeat.
This moment's regret,
that memory from a lost time,
are details, nothing more,

unable to obscure the full story
where, if not always heroic,
life moves forward
despite the rise and fall
of an uneven journey.

Happiness Is

a child who finds
a small brown box
and next to it, a red ribbon.
He excavates the waste bin
for scraps of white paper
        and crunches them
into the mouth of the box.
Then he buries the ribbon
deep inside until only
a small tip remains.
When asked what on earth
he intends to do with it,
the child smiles and says,
"Nothing. It's a dragon.
They do whatever they want."

Kindness

Kindness is a steady breeze
filling the sails of our efforts
to navigate a rough strait.

Kindness keeps us agile,
so we can step briskly
when expectations fall short.

Kindness instructs our hearts
to see with greater clarity
beyond what first appears.

Kindness is a gentle word
spoken in a moment
when speech turns brittle.

Speak True

We each carry a story,
more than one to be sure,
but one recurring story
holds the central theme.

Parts may hide in codicils,
in opinions and asides.
We hesitate to say it whole
for fear its gaps will show.

Our story leads us across
the uneven terrain of memory
with crumb-like clues
leading hopefully to a source.

We tell our story as best we can,
first to ourselves in silent times,
and aloud when courage invites
what only another can hear.

Pentimento

An artist before her easel
lays down a line of paint,

only later to scrape it off
to make way for another.

So each of us bears layers
of a story with many variations.

Each version gets closer to truth,
though truth itself shifts shape.

The version we now can tell
changes what we understand,

adding details we missed before
with colors more bold and honest.

Flawed Quest

Everything would be easier
if the road ran downhill,
if wind blew only from behind,
if it rained after midnight,
if temperatures were moderate,
if the ditches filled with blue iris,
if birds sang in harmony,
if doors never closed,
and bees never stung.

But the road rises twenty degrees,
and headwinds are made of steel.
Days pass wet and gray,
either too hot, too cold
or switch back and forth
        without warning.
The ditches fill with beer cans,
kitchen trash, and snubbed butts.
Along the fence a chorus of crows
croak some dirge over roadkill.
The exit is blocked with fallen debris,
and the alternate route is swamp.

If the messiness stalls you,
best to stay where you are,
though you may puzzle late at night -

if not now, then on your last night -
what wonder the flawed horizon held.

The Unfinished Life

So much will be left undone
as years slip by, as time
picks up its pace, marching
steadily to a now-near future.

So consider what you will do
in this precious hour, what joy
you will recognize, what sorrow
you will grieve once and for all.

Then walk into a field and sit
quietly in the caress of sunrise.
Breathe slowly to calm
the clamors of your heart.

What might have been, fades.
Let it go and hold no regret.
Lay claim to what lies ahead,
its beauty leading the way.

Sorrow's Journey

For Hannah McGraw-McDzik

Sorrow pulls up a heavy woolen cowl,
folds its hands into draped sleeves,
and walks the long, cold corridor of grief,
head down, its pace slow and measured.

Sorrow stops from time to time,
as though marking stations of the Cross.
At each stop, Sorrow sings a lament,
its voice rending the heart's silence.

Sorrow paces day and night,
the clip of footsteps a sharp cadence
piercing the fragile attempt at sleep
and its refuge from memory's haunts.

At a time unnamed, undated,
Sorrow slips out unnoticed.
What lingers is the echo of pacing
and the fading lyric of lament.

Shadow of Forgiveness

Sermons about forgiveness
issue a somber altar call
inviting our mind's assent.
We nod at its wisdom,
enumerate its benefits,
and agree to its practice.

We savor our new conviction
until it comes to a deep wound,
a wound that never healed –
a harbored slur, a broken trust,
a thoughtless betrayal that left
anger dormant in our bones.

This battle between mind and marrow
bewilders us who rely on reason
to keep to the righteous path
where our best selves prevail.
Not this sudden hardening of heart
and instant replay of resentment.

Forgiveness demands close attention,
a conscious act of choosing
day by day, moment by moment,
especially when a wound,
we long thought healed,
suddenly, surprisingly, re-opens.

Contemplation

The old woman sat on a stump,
her hands crossed in her lap
as she gazed across the yard.
It was not a blank stare,
unfocused and adrift.
She watched for signs of God,
for the movement of spirits
she believed wandered the earth.
She watched for flashes of beauty,
like the blue jay landing
among late summer beans,
becoming a small pool of water.

When she rose to leave,
there was no sigh of regret.
For she carried all she'd seen
in a tiny silk purse
       next to her heart.

Mistaken Identity

If you think a stone an apple,

why the shock when you break a tooth?

Or if you assume the locked door

a curtain of glass beads,

will the bump on your forehead

come as surprise or mystery?

When you pretend to be your false self,

will the deceit leave you embarrassed?

A butterfly cannot be a crow,

a pond has no claim to dry land,

and your soul, uniquely formed,

can only inhabit the history you are

and the body wherein it dwells.

Seeking Silence

We say we crave silence,
envy monks their cloisters,
places where sound
seldom rises above a decibel,
a single decibel soft as a breeze
and gentle enough to wait
hours for a response.

But we plug-in, log on,
Facebook, Tweet and text,
LinkIn and Snapchat,
churning up so much noise
we catch only snippets of words,
assuming a random collage
tells us all we need to know.

Noise has become an elixir
for loneliness, for the fear
we will be left alone
with no companions
except our memories,
and they tend to be
harsh conversationalists.

Rupert Brown

Rupert Brown came to the abbey
in his endless search
to find the serenity of heart
he longed for night and day.

He came to the abbey,
pockets stuffed with scriptures,
the seams of his valise strained
with tomes of learnéd answers.

He believed the abbey
would be the place of revelation,
its silence a welcome sanctuary
for what his soul needed most.

Rupert Brown arrived at the abbey,
was assigned a windowless room
over the kitchen where an irate cook
threw kettles against the wall.

He thought this might be a test,
one last step to sacred bliss
when a loud curse rose from below
so he took an early bus home.

A Misspent Life

He was not a loving man,
someone with opened arms,
but arms knotted and closed,
laced tight like a rucksack.
He read his Bible dutifully,
but snarled at his children
and anyone in his way.
His rigid jaw ached,
and his frown formed
a permanent scar.
He walked hunched over,
a man bearing bad news.

As he lay dying,
his wife stroked his hand,
asked him about God.
His doubt in mercy
caught her off guard.
She would have asked
questions to help him
find his way to peace,
but she learned long ago
it was better to keep silent.
And so she did,
        one last time.

Passage

For Dennis Callahan

Death closes the door,
      slams it shut
to make its cruel point.
The door will not open,
its hinges locked with rust
and its knob unturnable.
You stand before the door,
      lament and curse,
      demand it open.

So you are left
in this gray street of grief
looking to passersby
for any gesture, any word,
that might help you find
your way safely home.

The World's Wonder

Whose love finally wins our heart
has no common pattern.
It might strike like lightning,
the heavens suddenly afire,
charged air leaving us intoxicated,
our eyes dazzled by prismed light.

Or as often love reveals itself
                in the ordinary –
at the end of a long conversation,
a quiet walk along a winding path,
the casual touch of two hands.
For in the occurrences of daily life,
we discover a mysterious unfolding,
the graceful opening of hearts
filled with wonder at the simplest act.

Wisdom: An Instruction

For Roxanne DeLille

Wisdom can be found
in the most ordinary things,
like this small stone
you placed in my hand.
A smoothed bit of basalt,
born in fire, churned
by a roaring, mighty lake,
its size so forgettable.
Yet you placed it in my hand
to teach me resilience,
how in the mystery of creation
a small, homely stone
can bear with ease the weight
of even heart-breaking sorrow.

A Stay at the Shore

Asticou Inn, North Harbor, Maine

Chance brings me here
to a high porch above the sea,
a piano playing somewhere
in the elegant Asticou Inn
as light fades on a perfect day.

My grandfather, foreign born,
thought this is where he would be
once he stepped off the ship.
He imagined himself a man of means,
smoking cigars with his brandy
and giving no thought to the tab.

Instead, he got a hardscrabble farm,
prying from stony Wisconsin fields
barely enough to get by.
He'd sit on his stoop at night,
drunk on bootleg liquor,
and stare into the darkness.

He brooded over other people
sitting under the same dark sky,
but in high-polished chairs
overlooking a changing sea
as the day turned on its side
to embrace the night, unafraid.

No End In Sight

When humans discovered language,
words became a powerful tool
like the arrowhead, clay pot,
navigation by sun and stars.
With words, stories rose from the fire,
followed warriors into battle,
hunters into the dark forests,
planters and reapers into their fields.
Stories taught the fingers of artists,
filled the mouths of sages and priests,
and named all Earth's elements.
Words eased the mystery of death,
weaving narratives strong enough
to honor the weight of grief
and casting just enough light
to soothe impenetrable fear.

Facing Facts

How surprised you are
when the face in the mirror
is not yours but a crumpled replica,
even though the eyes are familiar,
and the crescent-shaped scar
from a mishap in first grade
look nearly the same.
A face maps a history,
and mine dates to 1945
when life was simple,
and I knew little of death.
But this impostor looks back,
with a bit of a smirk,
as though he's been waiting
for me to catch on to a truth
as obvious as a scar
curved like a crescent moon.

Presumption's Conceit

For so long this body ran on its own.
Joints moved smoothly,
muscles stretched and sprang back
with soundless ease.
After a short night with little sleep,
I could still bike twenty miles,
work all day without fatigue,
and stay up for the Late Show.
Gone. All those presumed functions,
running quietly in the background,
now need conscious tending
and the sort of pep talk
a preschool t-ball team needs.
Each day I tell myself calmly
the loss is only small when,
                    in fact,
            I know
it's a barefaced lie.

Memorial Poems

Poems for the dead recast truth,
for truth, after death, softens.
Who she was, who he sought to be,
        is told as midrash.

Too often judgment overcomes mercy.
We forget how much we can't see,
how much lies hidden,
        out of sight.

But Death sharpens our eyes
so we might notice finally
the small glowing light
        in the corner of every soul

where what matters in the end
finally steps into daylight
and, weighed in the balance
        is, at last, acclaimed.

First Draft

One word on a blank page,
written in a burst of passion
now sits, cooling.
Still it stirs curious thoughts
about songs it might sing
to rouse a sluggish mind.
With curiosity in the lead,
the pen follows double-time
building a house of words,
giving them some order,
so when linked together,
their bright colors and sounds
spark hope the page itself
                might catch fire.

A Sacrament of Words

Leaving behind the need
to be careful or clever,
our conversation turned,
　　　grew sacramental.
In the circle of friendship,
we encouraged each other to speak,
to stand daringly
on the edge of an idea,
　　　trusting gentle hands
were ready to bear us up
　　　as we learned to fly.

After Formalities

Nothing seems colder
than a room of strangers,
until someone speaks,
asks a question that kindles
a fire in the middle of the room
around which they gather
to warm their hands.

Anniversary Anthem
For Kathy, 2018

Not by chance does the seed,
in the dark cover of night,
suddenly break through the soil,
reaching greedily sunward.
Nor do Sandhill cranes just land
as though any place will do,
        knowing Nebraska is their oasis.
Fall folds into Winter and Winter
opens its arms to Spring, a balance
of death and life without a clock.
So in our unforeseen meeting,
we found gift and need aligned,
a longing met as though the gods
        certainly contrived it.

The Vision

Honoring Martin Luther King

We don't allow ourselves
to see visions so bold
we fall to our knees.
We grow accustomed
to cynicism, content to focus
on fault lines and gaps.

He told us to dream,
described a gracious landscape,
a place where ambiguity and dissent
could find reconciliation.
He cast light on fear, telling us
to draw closer, not flee.

He showed us how to stand
shoulder to shoulder
and face into the wind.
Despite his fears and failings,
he believed great possibility
took root in the deeds of good people -

a fact he consistently, constantly,
named as grace.

Wisdom

He was an old man.
He was a bent man,
his shoulders sloped
from long days in the field.
He was a quiet man.
He was a generous man,
his pockets emptied of coin
for beggars at the roadside.
He was a poor man,
a man without means,
wearied from hard labor.
He was an alert man.
He was a wise man
who read soul and sky as texts,
listening at dawn
for the morning's psalm.

Bright Star

For Linda Thain

The bright star you see
in the dark January sky
is no ordinary light.
It is where you need to look
when absence overwhelms
and the silence of your heart
empties your soul of music.
This star, spanning
what we know and what we don't,
tells of the unbroken cord
linking soul to soul
between the land of the living
and the land where all life
draws its light,
a promise exceeding
our Earth-bound imaginations.

Getting My Attention

Tell me something
to turn my head –
not flattery,
for age has tempered
my need for false praise.
Make it about stars,
their orbits and long falls
lasting centuries.
Such things open my eyes,
temper my need to know
the outcome of this day's
clamor and urgencies
so I might delight
in the ribbon of dust
dancing on morning light.

Unlearned Lesson

No one would be indifferent
coming upon a man
who kept walking into the same
                        barred door.
They would think him foolish
not to see the door was locked.

But we forget such common sense
when we enter our secret room,
ready once more to rehearse
a story and its predictable ending,
imagining this time it might
            come out differently.

Called To See

In Honor of Thomas Fisch, Teacher

It seemed simple enough, at first:
images of light and darkness
telling the world's story.
But soon images in thousands
          jostled for attention,
crowding out a vision
          pure and clear.

Then it was we turned
to those with imaginations
          honed on wonder,
on wisdom gained from other men,
          from other women,
whose angles of sight cast light
where obscurity prevailed.

We sought those whose convictions
          lifted our eyes
to see beyond what was near at hand.
We received welcome from these
for whom the act of seeing
          was at heart communion.
We called them friends,
companions for the journey,
and we called them
   – eyes wide with awe –
   teachers.

The Sum of All Things
For Carol Rennie OSB

When life takes a detour,
leaving us nearly stranded
in a place strange and new,
we may feel a surge of panic.
But as we grow still,
another route opens
as we sight a star we know,
leading where destiny calls.
On the journey that beckons,
we are ever the explorer,
knowing the call we hear
simply sets a direction.
What happens next requires
our close attention,
help from companions,
and trust in Wisdom's lead.

Conversation

We've learned each other's syntax,
how questions open up ideas we lift
together toward the light.
Whatever is said finds welcome,
           not as oracle,
but as the way we sharpen
the edge of a thought.
We offer lines to each other,
move them around,
and sometimes we let them go,
their purpose served in leading us
           to a clearer view,
so when next we meet,
we might pick up
right where we left off -
           but far more wise.

Daily Morning Mass

These elders come every day,
settle on arthritic knees
to say prayers dog-eared by time.
Some come with prayer books,
antiques from another age.
Some come only with their beads,
their fingering a language of its own.
Prayers come from deep within,
releasing words in breaths
         rising heavenward
like small clouds of incense.

Cemetery Travelogue

Cemeteries are tidy places.
laid out in straight, trim lines,
a final irony especially
for those whose lives ran
crooked and disheveled.

Cemeteries gather the dead,
give them their own territory
so their spirits can roam free,
knowing their incorruptible names
have a final mailing address.

Cemeteries are not sad places,
except for those who come
seeking what was left unspoken
and finding, to their regret,
a cold, wordless silence.

Calvary Cemetery
Faribault Minnesota

Here lie the Murphys,
there some Zimmermans,
along the fence Cloutiers,
and beyond them the Duchenes
    in their multitude.
In this village of bones, status
no longer matters or counts
though some scattered markers
make one last try to stand out.

But now comes Manuel Pasuelos,
late to town and recently dead.
He rests amidst Stassens,
    Chavies, and Dulacs.
His gravestone in Spanish
announces a new democracy
imposed by Death, in whose province
everyone ends up the same.

The Imperfect Teacher

My father taught me little –
not how to fish, hold a bat,
fix the brakes,
talk to women.
When men tell me
what they learned from their fathers,
I feel the sting of regret,
what seems a lost birthright.

My father taught me little
about manual arts
or how human beings relate,
but he schooled me
in how a person's word
should mean something,
how belief in God rings dull
without living proof in kindness.

My father taught in his own way,
with lessons I would someday grasp
when I was ready to be instructed,
when my resistance to him softened,
and when my need for his perfection
faded.

Unbreakable Bond

We remember the dead.
Their faces line our dreams
or catch our eye in the slant of light
at the end of a lonesome day.

We carry them like a talisman,
a carved piece of sorrow
worn smooth by its handling,
rough edges slowly rounded.

In time we learn to walk
with the grief of their leaving,
the traces of their memory
part of our unspoken comfort.

For our dead surround us
in this churning sea we still sail,
their faces our North Star,
our bond obscured, never broken.

Where Are You?

A Memorial For Mary Ann

Where are you when I need you,
when I need to know
what only you can recall?
When I want to hear a voice
filled with love, not judgment?
When I puzzle over a history
we share, made better by you?

We never agreed that you
would return in a dream
and offer me advice I needed,
even if it annoyed me.
But I trusted you'd not forget
how much I fret and stew,
losing perspective and balance.

But nights pass with you absent.
So today, the day of your birth,
I make my request quite plain.
The world continues without you.
Seasons turn, we all "moved on,"
but none of us are quite the same,
which makes your visit urgent.

The Narrator

In memory of Kieran Nolan OSB

He tells his story
in handfuls of words
he pulls from a memory
more clouded each day.
He remains undaunted
when a thread he holds
slips away, leaving him
empty-handed and adrift.
He simply asks for a word,
a clue, and the fog clears.
With forgotten details in hand,
he re-constructs a story
that helps map a life
he embraced as adventure
and now gives him solace
          in its recalling.

Last Vision

The last thing he saw
before he closed his eyes
one final time
was a bright aurora,
a brilliant display of yellow,
magenta, blue, and green.
He would have gasped,
surprised by such beauty,
had he not come to see
how his entire life
was becoming fire and light
and, at long last, peace.

CPSIA information can be obtained
at www.ICGtesting.com
Printed in the USA
BVHW041847100322
631168BV00014B/491

9 781093 635416